FLANNE
PACIFIC NORTHWEST
COOKBOOK

Food from Alaska,
Oregon and Washington

Second Edition

By Tim Murphy

Copyright 2015
Shamrock Arrow Media

For information on Flannel John's Cookbooks for Guys, upcoming releases and merchandise visit www.flanneljohn.com

FLANNEL JOHN'S PACIFIC NORTHWEST COOKBOOK

Food from Alaska, Oregon and Washington
Second Edition

<u>Table of Contents</u>

ABALONE CHOWDER

6 abalone fillets, thin and diced
3 cups of milk
1½ cup of hot water
4 slices of bacon, diced
1 potato, peeled and diced
1 onion, diced fine
1 tablespoon of butter
Salt and pepper to taste

In a large pan, cook bacon until halfway crisp. Drain off all but 2 tablespoon of the bacon grease. Add the diced fish, potato and onion to the pan until all are browned. Add hot water and simmer until potatoes are tender. In a second pan heat milk and butter then combine both mixtures. Stir and warm and add salt and pepper to taste.

APPLE-RAISIN CHUTNEY

2 tart apples, peeled, cored and diced
½ cup of raisins
½ cup of brown sugar
¼ cup of apple cider vinegar
¼ cup of onion, diced
¼ cup of water
1 teaspoon of turmeric
½ teaspoon of ginger
¼ teaspoon of salt
¼ teaspoon of ginger
Cloves to taste

For this recipe, fresh ground spices yield the best results. Combine all ingredients in a pan and cook over medium heat for 20 to 25 minutes. Stir the mixture occasionally. Once it reaches a boil, reduce heat to a simmer. Let the mixture cool and cover. Refrigerate overnight.

APPLES & YAMS

4 yams, cooked and sliced
2 large apples, peeled, cored and sliced
1 cup of sugar
3 tablespoons of cornstarch
2 cups of water
1 stick of butter
2 teaspoons of lemon juice

In a pan combine cornstarch and sugar then stir in water, butter and lemon juice. Heat and stir until it thickens. Place yams and apples in a baking dish and pour sauce over them. Bales at 350 degrees for 40 minutes are until apples are tender.

BAKED CLAMS

1 pint of clams, cleaned
1 cup of dry bread crumbs
½ cup of Cheddar cheese, grated
½ cup of oil
1 tablespoon of onion, diced
1 teaspoon of salt

Mix oil salt and onion thoroughly. Place clams in the mixture for 1 minute. Remove clams from the liquid and drain. Roll clams in cheese and then in breadcrumbs. Place clams in a well-greased baking dish and bake at 450 degrees for 12 minutes or until lightly browned.

BAKED HALIBUT

2 pounds of halibut fillets
1 cup of sour cream
½ cup of green onion, diced
¼ cup of Parmesan cheese, grated
1 teaspoon of dill weed
Salt and pepper to taste
Butter

Put fish in a well-buttered baking dish. Mix sour cream, green onion and dill weed and pour over the halibut. Season with salt and pepper. Bake at 350 degrees for 20 to 25 minutes. Sprinkle cheese over the top and broil until cheese is slightly browned.

BAKED OYSTERS

1 quart of oysters
1 cup of cornmeal or bread crumbs
2 eggs, slightly beaten
2 tablespoons of milk
1 teaspoon of salt
Pepper to taste (usually ¼ teaspoon or less)

Drain the liquid from the oysters. Mix eggs, milk and seasonings thoroughly. Dip oysters in the egg mixture and roll in cornmeal or breadcrumbs. Place on a cookie sheet or baking dish. Bake at 450 degrees for 15 minutes.

BAKED ROCKFISH

4 rockfish fillets, cleaned
2 tablespoons of lemon juice, fresh squeezed
½ cup of Parmesan cheese, freshly grated
3 tablespoons of scallions, diced
3 tablespoons of mayonnaise
2 tablespoons of sour cream

Place fillets in a baking dish and sprinkle with lemon juice. Mix the rest of ingredients in a bowl then spread mixture on the fish. Bake for 15 to 18 minutes or until fish is opaque.

BAKED SCALLOPS

1 pound of scallops
1 cup of cracker crumbs
½ cup of cream
2 tablespoons of butter, melted
Salt and pepper
Nutmeg

Mix scallops with cream. Add salt, pepper and nutmeg to taste and ¾ cup of the cracker crumbs. Place in a baking dish and sprinkle remaining crumbs on top. Drizzle with melted butter. Bake at 375 degrees for 25 minutes.

BAKED PEARS

3 pears, peeled, cored and sliced in half
½ cup of orange liqueur
2 tablespoons of brown sugar
2 tablespoons of cardamom, ground

When you slice the pears, leave the halves slightly attached, to look like butterfly wings. Put them in a baking dish. Sprinkle fruit with brown sugar then pour liqueur over them and finish with a sprinkle of cardamom. Bake at 350 degrees for 40 minutes or until the fruit is tender.

BARBECUED SALMON

5-pound salmon
   (cleaned with head & tail removed)
1 cup of barbecue sauce
2 slices of onion, thick
Salt and pepper to taste

Place fish on a large, heavy piece of aluminum foil or double fold if needed. Stuff the fish with 2 onion slices and salt and pepper to taste. Pour barbecue sauce over the fish and securely wrap the foil so sauce will not leak out. Grill over hot coal and slowly cook for 75 to 90 minutes.

BEAR JERKY

4 pounds of bear meat cut into strips
1 quart of water
¼ cup of Morton Tender Quick
   or curing salt
½ cup of brown sugar
1 tablespoon of black pepper
1 tablespoon of granulated garlic

In a large bowl mix water, salt, sugar, pepper and garlic. Stir until sugar and salt are dissolved. Add bear meat and mix thoroughly. Cover and refrigerate for 8 to 10 hours. Keep the meat completely covered in the marinade. You can switch up the spices in the marinade and try onion powder, lemon pepper, cayenne pepper or teriyaki sauce. Take meat out of the fridge but do not rinse. Pat dry or place on a rack to air dry for 1 hour. Bake in an oven between 150 and 175 degrees overnight or dry according to your dehydrator or smoker's directions. If using a smoker, try to keep the temperature between 150 and 200 degrees. When jerky is done, let cool in a baking dish or bowl covered in plastic wrap. The jerky can be refrigerated and frozen for extended storage.

BEAR STEW

4 pounds of bear meat, cubed
4 cups of all-purpose flour
1 teaspoon of oregano
1 teaspoon of salt
1 teaspoon of black pepper
4 tablespoons of butter
2 tablespoons of olive oil
2½ quarts of water
1 onion, chopped
1 cup of beef broth
4 bay leaves (remove after cooking)
2 pounds of red potatoes, cubed
1 pound of mushrooms (fresh or canned)
5 carrots, sliced

In a large bowl, combine flour, oregano, salt and pepper. Heat butter and oil in a large skillet over medium heat. Coat the bear meat in the flour mixture and add to hot oil. Fry meat until browned. Remove and drain on paper towels. In a large pot or Dutch oven, add water and all ingredients. Stir well. Cook over medium-low heat for 2 to 3 hours stirring occasionally and adding water if needed.

BLUEBERRY SYRUP

2 cups of blueberries
1 cup of sugar
½ cup of water

Combine all ingredients in a pan. Boil until the berries are soft then strain mixture through a sieve. Pour into a jar or bottle and seal.

BROWN SUGAR SALMON

2 salmon fillets
1 cup of brown sugar
1 stick of butter
½ cup of green onions, diced
¼ teaspoon of dry mustard

In a pan melt butter over low heat then stir in brown sugar until it dissolves then add dry mustard. Place salmon fillets skin side down on aluminum foil. Glaze the fish with the brown sugar mixture. Place the foil and fish under a broiler for 5 to 7 minutes. When fish is almost done, apply a second layer of the glaze and sprinkle with green onions. Broil for another 1 to 2 minutes.

CANTALOUPE MINT SUMMER SOUP

    2 ripe cantaloupes, peeled, seeded and cut
        into chunks
    ½ cup of orange juice, not from concentrate
    2 tablespoons of fresh mint leaves, chopped
    2 tablespoons of sugar
    4 tablespoons of sour cream

Puree cantaloupe, mint and sugar in a blender or food processor until sugar dissolves. Pour mixture into a ceramic bowl. Whisk in sour cream and orange juice. Put mixture in a bowl, cover and chill overnight.

CARIBOU TERIYAKI

2 pounds of caribou meet
¼ cup of soy sauce
3 tablespoons of brown sugar
½ cup of water
1 teaspoon of ground ginger
1 teaspoon of garlic powder
¼ teaspoon of pepper
Oil

Slice meat into ¼-inch thick strips. Mix all ingredients together and marinate the meat in the sauce for 3 hours in a cool place or overnight in a refrigerator or on ice. Remove meat from marinade and fry in a skillet in a little oil.

CLAM CASSEROLE

18 ounces of clamed, minced and drained
18 saltine crackers, coarsely crushed
4 eggs, well beaten
½ cup of milk
½ cup of onion, diced
¼ cup of green pepper, diced
¼ cup of butter, melted
1 teaspoon of salt

Mix all ingredients thoroughly and pour into a well-buttered slow cooker. Cook on low for 4 to 5 hours.

CLAM CHOWDER

1 pint of clams with liquid
20 ounces of tomatoes, canned or fresh
½ cup of bacon, diced
1 onion, diced
2 cups of potatoes, diced
2 cups of water
1 teaspoon of salt
¼ teaspoon of pepper (or less)
¼ teaspoon of thyme (or less)
1 bay leaf

Sauté bacon in a large pot until crisp. Add in the onion and fry for 5 minutes. Add potato, bay leaf and water. Simmer for 10 to 15 minutes or until potatoes are cooked. Add in the remaining ingredients to the pot. Heat and stir the mixture, but do not boil.

CLAM FRITTERS

24 clams, chopped
2 cups of flour
2 eggs
1 cup of milk
½ cup of clam juice
2 teaspoons of baking powder
½ teaspoon of salt
Pepper to taste

Sift the dry ingredients than add milk, clam juice and eggs. Mix thoroughly then stir in chopped clams. Drop spoonfuls onto a well-greased griddle or skillet. Fry until golden brown.

CLOVER WINE

1 gallon of clover blossoms
1 gallon of boiling water
3 pounds of sugar
3 oranges, sliced
3 lemons, sliced
2 tablespoons of active dry yeast

In a large completely clean container (no bacteria) place clover blossoms. Pour boiling water over the blossoms, loosely cover and let rest for 3 days. Strain the liquid through cheesecloth or fine mesh and mix with oranges, lemons, sugar and yeast. Place the liquid in a glass or ceramic container. Cover with cheesecloth and let stand at room temperature for 3 weeks. Strain the liquid again and pour into clean, sterilized bottles then seal.

CRAB DRESSING

1 quart of mayonnaise
1 cup of chili sauce
½ cup of celery, diced
½ cup of hard-boiled egg, chopped
½ cup of olives

Mix thoroughly, chill if you prefer and then serve.

CRAB-IN-A-BLANKET

½ pound of crab meat, flaked
8 ounces of cream cheese
¼ cup of celery, diced
¼ cup of toasted almonds, chopped
1 tablespoon of parsley, chopped fine
1 tablespoon of lemon juice
12 thin ham slices
Salt and pepper

Mix crab with all ingredients except ham. Spread mixture on ham slices, roll, and secure with a toothpick. Chill for at least 6 hours. Remove toothpicks before serving.

CRAB MELTS

8 ounces of crabmeat
4 English muffins, separated in halves
8 slices of Monterey Jack cheese
1 cup of mayonnaise
2 green onions, diced fine

Mix crabmeat with mayonnaise and onion. Toast the English muffins and spread crab mixture on each half. Top with a cheese slice and broil until cheese melts and becomes bubbly.

CRAB SOUP

8 ounces of crabmeat, chunked
2 eggs, hard-boiled and separated
1 can of cream of celery soup
1 cup of milk
1 cup of cream
3 teaspoons of sherry
1 tablespoon of butter
1 tablespoon of flour
1 teaspoon of parsley, minced
1 teaspoon of fresh lemon zest
Salt and pepper to taste

In a pot melt butter then stir in flour followed by soup, milk, cream and crumbled egg yolks. Stir thoroughly and heat without boiling. Add the crabmeat to the pot and heat for 10 minutes. Stir in sherry, crumbled egg whites, lemon zest, parsley, salt and pepper.

CRANBERRY APPLESAUCE

1 can of jellied cranberry sauce
½ cup of applesauce
¼ teaspoon of cinnamon

Combine all ingredients thoroughly and chill for 3 hours.

CRANBERRY CHUTNEY

1 cup of cranberries
1 onion, sliced in quarters
1 green pepper, sliced in quarters
1 apple, peeled, cored and quartered
½ cup of sugar
½ cup of apple cider vinegar
¾ teaspoon of salt

Put cranberries, onion, green pepper and apple in a blender or food processor. Chop coarsely. In a pan, combine cranberry mixture with sugar, vinegar and salt. Bring to a boil, reduce heat, cover and simmer for 10 minutes. Cool and refrigerate.

CRANBERRY CHICKEN

1 chicken, in pieces
1 package of dry onion soup mix
15 ounces of cranberry sauce
12 ounces of French dressing

Place chicken pieces in a lightly greased baking dish. Mix remaining ingredients together and pour over chicken pieces. Bake at 350 degrees for 55 to 65 minutes.

CRANBERRY TEA

1 pound of fresh cranberries
3 quarts of water
Juice from 3 lemons
Juice from 1 orange
2½ cups of sugar
2 cinnamon sticks
1 teaspoon of whole cloves

Boil cranberries in a large pot with water until the berries pop. Add in remaining ingredients and simmer for 30 minutes. Strain and serve hot.

CRAYFISH BOIL

1 gallon of water
½ cup of salt
Live crawfish
Chilled water

Add salt to 1 gallon of water and bring to a boil. Drop in live crawfish. When water returns to a boil, let it go for 2 to 3 minutes. You will know when the crawfish are cooked when they turn bright red. Remove them immediately and drop them in chilled water. This makes the shell easier to remove. Clean before eating.

CRAYFISH STEW

2 pounds of crayfish tails
1½ cups of water
3 tablespoons of oil
2 onions, diced
2 stalks of celery, diced
½ cup of tomato sauce
½ green pepper, diced
½ clove or garlic, minced
2 tablespoons of flour
1 tablespoon of Worcestershire sauce
¼ teaspoon of hot sauce
Salt and pepper to taste

Heat oil in a pot. Add onion, green pepper, celery and garlic. Sauté until clear. Add water, crayfish, flour, tomato sauce, hot sauce, Worcestershire sauce, salt and pepper. Simmer over low heat for 30 to 35 minutes.

CREAM OF CRAB SOUP

1 quart of milk
¼ stick of butter
½ cup of flour
1 pound of crabmeat
Salt and pepper

Mix flour with just enough water to make a paste. In a pan combine paste with milk and butter and stir over low heat until thick and smooth. Stir in the crabmeat and season with salt and pepper. Stir and heat until the liquid begins to bubble.

CRUSTED HALIBUT

4 6-ounce halibut fillets, cleaned
1 cup of macadamia nuts, ground
1 tablespoon of olive oil
¼ teaspoon of dried thyme

Combine the macadamia nut pieces with olive oil and thyme. Paint the mixture on top of the fish fillets. Put the fish in a baking dish and bake at 450 degrees for 10 to 12 minutes until the centers are opaque.

DEER HUNTER'S CHILI

3 small cans of kidney beans
4 small cans of crushed stewed tomatoes
8 garlic cloves, chopped
6 jalapenos with stems removed
  (3 diced without seeds)
1 red bell pepper, chopped
1 green bell pepper, chopped
1 pound of ground venison
1 pound of pork (or Italian sausage)
1 yellow onion, chopped
¼ bunch of cilantro
¾ tablespoon of oregano
¾ tablespoon of basil
¾ tablespoon of chili powder
1 tablespoon of salt
1 teaspoon of black pepper

Brown your meats of choice meat and drain. Add seasonings and vegetables and cook for 10 minutes on medium heat. Add tomatoes and beans, adjusting tomatoes to thin or thicken mixture. Cook until beans and vegetables are soft. The longer and slower it's cooked, the better it tastes.

DUNGENESS CRAB BURGER

1½ cups of Dungeness crabmeat pieces
2 hard-boiled eggs, chopped
4 cheddar cheese slices
3 ounces of mayonnaise
3 ounces of chili sauce
3 tablespoons of olives, chopped
Juice from ½ lemon
4 hamburger buns

Combine crabmeat with egg, mayonnaise, chili sauce, olives and lemon juice. Mix thoroughly. Spread mixture on split hamburger buns, place on a broiler pan and broil for 5 to 7 minutes. Top with a slice of cheddar cheese and return to broiler until cheese is melted.

DUNGENESS CRAB SAUCE

1 cup of mayonnaise
1 cup of chili sauce
¼ cup of celery, diced fine
4 sprigs of parsley, chopped fine
2 scallions, diced fine
1 tablespoon of lemon juice
1 tablespoon of sugar
1 teaspoon of Worcestershire sauce

Combine all ingredients thoroughly and refrigerate for at least 3 hours.

ELK CHILI

2 pounds of ground elk
2 pounds of tomatoes, diced (fresh or canned)
1 onion, diced
1 bell pepper, diced
6 ounces of tomato paste
1 cup of water
1 can of kidney beans
½ teaspoon of garlic powder
2 teaspoons of salt
2 teaspoons of Italian seasoning
2 teaspoons of chili powder
2 teaspoons of pepper

Brown meat in a skillet. Put meat and the rest of the ingredients in a pot. Cover and simmer at a low temperature for 45 to 60 minutes.

FINNISH CRAWFISH

1 gallon of water
½ cup of salt
2 tablespoons of dill, fresh or dried
Live crawfish
Cold water

Add salt and dill to 1 gallon of water and bring to a boil for 4 minutes. Drop in live crawfish. When water returns to a boil, let it go for 2 to 3 minutes. Crawfish are cooked when they turn bright red. Remove them immediately and plunge them into cold water. This makes the shell easier to remove. Clean before eating.

FISH & SHRIMP BEER BATTER

1½ cups of flour
½ cup of cornmeal
12 ounces of beer
1 tablespoon of paprika
1 tablespoon of salt

In the first bowl mix cornmeal and ½ cup of flour. In a second bowl mix beer, 1 cup of flour, paprika and salt and whisk. Dip fish or shrimp in the beer mixture then in the cornmeal mixture. Fry in oil.

FISH MARINADE

½ cup of rice vinegar
½ cup of lime juice, fresh squeezed
¼ cup of oil
1 tablespoon of honey
1 tablespoon of chili oil
1 teaspoon of sesame seed

Mix all ingredients thoroughly and store in bottle that can be sealed.

FISHERMAN'S CATCH CHOWDER

16 ounces of tomatoes, fresh or canned
½ pound of ocean perch
½ pound of halibut
½ pound of catch of the day, your choice
8 ounces of clam juice
½ cup of dry white wine
½ cup of onion, chopped
½ cup of celery, diced
½ cup of carrots, diced
¼ cup of cream
3 tablespoons of flour
3 tablespoons of butter, melted
1 teaspoon of salt
¼ teaspoon of rosemary

Cut cleaned fish into 1-inch chunks. Combine all of the ingredients except flour, butter and cream, in a slow cooker and stir well. Cover and cook on low for 6 to 8 hours. One hour before serving, combine cream, flour and butter and stir into the fish mixture.

FRIED HALIBUT

2 pounds of halibut pieces
1 cup of fine breadcrumbs
  (cracker or cornmeal)
1 egg
1 tablespoon of milk
1 teaspoon of salt
Pepper to taste
Oil

Fish should be in bite-sized chunks. Sprinkle pieces with salt and pepper. Blend the egg with milk. Dip fish in the egg mixture then roll in crumbs. Cook fish in a deep fryer with oil at 375 degrees for 3 to 5 minutes or until golden brown. In a fry pan, cook 3 to 5 minutes per side until golden brown.

FRIED OYSTERS

1 quart of oysters
1 cup of breadcrumbs
(cracker crumbs, cornmeal or cracker crumbs)
2 eggs, beaten
2 tablespoons of milk
1 teaspoon of salt
Pepper to taste
Oil

Drain oysters. Mix eggs, milk and seasonings thoroughly. Dip oysters in the egg mixture and roll in crumbs. In a deep fryer or skillet, fry spoonfuls of the oysters in oil. When they brown on one side flip and brown the other side. Cooking time is 4 to 6 minutes.

GINGER CARROT SOUP

2½ cups of chicken broth
2 cups of carrots, sliced ½-inch thick
1 stalk of celery, sliced ½-inch thick
½ cup of onion, diced
1 tablespoon of fresh ginger, grated
Salt and pepper

Place carrots, celery, onion and broth in a pan. Bring ingredients to a boil then reduce to a low simmer, cover, and let cook for 30 minutes. Put entire mixture in a blender or food processor and puree. Add ginger plus salt and pepper to taste. Return to pan and heat and stir for a few more minutes to blend flavors.

GRILLED CHEESE & PEAR SANDWICH

Sour Dough Bread (or your favorite)
Butter or Margarine
Sliced Sharp Cheddar
Sliced Havarti
Mayonnaise
Creamy Horse Radish Sauce
Bacon Bits
French's French Fried Onions
Pear Jam or Preserves
(peach or apricot can work too)

For each sandwich butter one side of each slice of bread. On the other, spread one with a mixture of mayonnaise and horseradish sauce and one with the pear jam. Then between the 2 slices, add a slice of each cheese, bacon bits and French fried onions. Close and fry in pan until golden brown and cheese has melted.

GRILLED SALMON

4 salmon fillets, cleaned (6 to 8 ounces each)
1 tablespoon of olive oil
½ tablespoon of granulated garlic
Salt and fresh ground pepper

Rub the salmon with olive oil, then season with garlic, salt and pepper. Place salmon on a hot grill for 3 to 5 minutes per side. There should be just a hint of translucence in the center when they're done.

HALIBUT STEAKS

1½ pounds of halibut steaks
1 small onion, sliced into rings
½ cup of sour cream
½ cup of Cheddar cheese, grated
¼ stick of butter, melted
Juice from ½ lemon
Salt and pepper
Garlic salt (optional)

Place fish in a baking dish and season with salt and pepper. Top fish with onion rings. Mix sour cream, melted butter and lemon juice. Thoroughly. Pour the sauce over the halibut. Sprinkle the cheese on top. Sprinkle with garlic salt. Bake at 350 degrees for 30 minutes, uncovered.

HOMEMADE APPLE SAUCE

10 apples, peeled, cored and sliced
½ cup of water
½ cup of sugar
½ cup of brown sugar
2 tablespoons of cinnamon
1 teaspoon of nutmeg
½ teaspoon of ground cloves
1 tablespoon of butter
2 tablespoons of lemon juice

Place ingredients in the cooker and stir thoroughly. Cover and cook on low for 8 to 10 hours. Chill the sauce upon completion or spoon the warm mixture on vanilla ice cream.

HONEY GINGERED CARROTS

1 ½ pounds of carrots, sliced
2 tablespoons of honey
2 tablespoons of butter
½ teaspoon salt
¼ teaspoons of ginger
Pinch of cinnamon

Put carrots in boiling salted water for 12 to 15 minutes until tender. Mix remaining ingredients together in a separate bowl to make a sauce. Remove carrots from the water and pour the sauce over them.

ITALIAN HALIBUT

1 pound of halibut fillets
1½ cups of tomato sauce
¼ cup of Parmesan cheese

Place fish in a baking dish and pour the sauce over the fish. Sprinkle Parmesan cheese over the sauce and fish. Bake at 350 degrees for 30 minutes or until fish is firm.

KETCHIKAN TARTAR SAUCE

1 cup of mayonnaise
2 teaspoons of lemon juice
1 tablespoon of sweet pickles, diced
1 tablespoon of parsley, diced fine
1 tablespoon of onion, diced fine

Mix thoroughly and serve. You may want to chill for a few hours depending on your taste.

LAMB KABOBS

2 pounds of lamb, cut in bite-sized cubes
5 cloves of garlic, minced
2 tablespoons of olive oil
2 tablespoons of ketchup
Salt and pepper to taste

Mix together ketchup garlic, ketchup, olive oil, salt and pepper to taste. Marinate the meat in the sauce for 2 hours in the refrigerator. Place meat on skewers. Grill over coals, on a gas grill or in a broiler until done to taste. For different flavors, you can substitute yogurt for ketchup and beef for lamb.

LAMB MARINADE

½ cup of olive oil
½ cup of red wine vinegar
3 cloves of garlic, minced
2 teaspoons of Dijon mustard
½ teaspoon of dry thyme
½ teaspoon of dry rosemary
½ teaspoon of dry oregano
1 tablespoon of soy sauce
1 tablespoon of dry sherry
1 teaspoon of salt
½ teaspoon of black pepper, freshly ground

Combine all ingredients thoroughly. In a bowl, cover meat with the marinade, cover bowl and refrigerate for 6 to 24 hours. The longer it marinates, the more intense the flavor.

LAMB SHANKS

4 thick-cut lamb shanks
16 ounces of tomato sauce
½ cup of brown sugar
1 onion, sliced thin
1 clove of garlic
1 teaspoon of dill
1 teaspoon of rosemary
½ teaspoon of oregano

Brown the shanks in a skillet. Mix the remaining ingredients and pour half the mixture into the pan. Place the shanks on the top and cover with the rest of the mixture. Cover and bake at 300 degrees for 3 hours. Uncover and continue to cook for 30 minutes. Recipe can also be done is a slow cooker.

LEMON BAKED COD

1 pound of cod fillets
¼ cup of butter, melted
¼ cup of flour
2 tablespoons of lemon
½ teaspoon of salt
¼ teaspoon of pepper
Paprika

Cut fish into bite-sized chunks. In a small bowl, mix butter and lemon juice. In a second bowl, mix flour, salt and pepper. Dip fish pieces in butter mixture followed by the flour mixture. Place fish in an ungreased baking dish. Pour remaining butter mixture over the fish and sprinkle with paprika. Bake at 350 degrees for 24 to 28 minutes or until fish flakes easily.

MEAT MARINADE

¼ cup of red wine vinegar
1 clove of garlic, minced
3 tablespoons of Dijon mustard
2 tablespoons of olive oil
2 teaspoons of brown sugar
1 teaspoon of black pepper, freshly ground
½ teaspoon of salt
½ teaspoon of dry thyme
½ teaspoon of dry rosemary

Combine all ingredients in a non-metallic bowl. This recipe works for beef, venison, elk and moose.

MINT SAUCE FOR LAMB

½ cup of mint jelly
2 tablespoons of Merlot wine
1 teaspoon of white wine vinegar
1 tablespoon of fresh mint, minced

In a bowl, whisk together jelly, wine and vinegar thoroughly. Add fresh mint add serve

MOM'S FISH LOAF

2 cups of fish, cooked
1 cup of cooked carrots, coarsely mashed
¾ cup of hot milk
2 cups of soft bread crumbs, no crust
2 eggs, beaten
2 tablespoons of celery, diced
2 tablespoons of green pepper, diced
2 tablespoons of onion, diced
2 tablespoons of parsley, chopped
1 teaspoon of salt
Pepper

Mix together breadcrumbs, fish, eggs, milk and pepper. Add remaining ingredients and form mixture into a loaf pan. Bake at 375 degrees for 45 minutes or until it tests for doneness.

MOOSE HASH

1½ pounds of cooked moose steak, diced
½ pound of bacon, diced
½ onion, diced
2 large potatoes, cooked and diced
4 eggs, poached
1 stick of butter
Salt and pepper

Melt butter in a skillet. Mix moose, bacon, onion and potatoes thoroughly and fry in butter until golden brown and crisp. Salt and pepper to taste. Put on a platter and topped with poached eggs.

MOOSE STEW

2 pounds moose, cubed
20 ounces of tomatoes (canned or fresh)
1 box of frozen peas
6 sliced carrots
3 small chopped onions
1 cup of diced celery
3 medium potatoes diced
5 ounces of chestnuts, sliced and drained
¼ cup of red wine
2 tablespoons of sugar
1 tablespoon of salt
¼ teaspoon of pepper

Combine all ingredients thoroughly in a baking dish and cover. Bake at 275 degrees for 5 hours.

MUSHROOM SALAD

½ pound of fresh mushrooms, sliced thin
¼ cup of scallions, sliced thin
3 tablespoons of olive oil
2 teaspoons of fresh lemon juice
½ teaspoon of salt

In a bowl toss mushrooms with lemon juice until slightly moist. Add in scallion, oil and salt and toss again. Chill for at least 2 hours.

OREGON TRAIL GRANOLA

3 cups of rolled oats
¾ cup of raisins
½ cup of sweetened coconut, shredded
½ cup of almonds, sliced
¼ cup of wheat germ
¼ cup of honey
¼ cup of seeds or nuts of choice (optional)
¼ cup of vegetable oil
2½ tablespoons of water
2 tablespoons of brown sugar
¾ teaspoon of vanilla extract
¼ teaspoon of salt

In bowl #1, mix oats, coconut, almonds, wheat germ and seeds/nuts of choice. In bowl #2, mix honey, oil, water, brown sugar, vanilla and salt. Now pour the wet mixture over the dry mixture and coat thoroughly. Spread the granola mixture on a baking sheet and bake at 350 degrees for 25 minutes. Lightly stir granola every 5 minutes to bake evenly. Mixture is done when it's golden brown. Be careful not to burn.

OYSTER STEW

1 pint of fresh oysters with liquid
1 can of evaporated milk
1 can of water
2 tablespoons of butter
1 tablespoon of Worcestershire sauce
1 teaspoon of salt
Dash of pepper

In a pan cook oysters in their liquid for about 3 minutes or until the edges curl. Pour in can of milk and a can of water and heat to just before boiling but do not boil. Add Worcestershire sauce to the stew then remove from heat. Stir in butter and serve.

PAN FRIED SMELT

2 pounds of smelt, cleaned
½ cup of corn meal
½ cup of flour
1 tablespoon of salt
½ teaspoon of pepper
Water
Oil or butter

Mix cornmeal, flour, salt and pepper thoroughly. Dip smelt in water than coat with the cornmeal mixture. In a skillet, fry in oil or butter for 4 to 5 minutes per side or until nicely browned.

PEAR PIE

2 9-inch pie crusts, unbaked
4 pears, peeled and sliced in quarters
¾ cup of sugar
½ cup of cream
1 egg
2 level tablespoons of cornstarch
Pinch of crushed cloves

Line pie tin with 1 crust. Fill with quartered pears. Combine egg, sugar, cornstarch, cream and cloves thoroughly and pour over pears. Top with the second piecrust. Bake at 425 degrees for 15 minutes then reduce to 350 degrees for 30 minutes.

RAZOR CLAM CHOWDER

1 pint of razor clams with liquid
1 quart of milk
4 potatoes, diced
1 onion, finely diced
4 sliced of bacon, diced
Salt and pepper to taste

Fry bacon until golden brown and drain the grease. Add the bacon to the clams. In a pot, brown onion slightly then add clams, bacon and potatoes. Cover with water and simmer until potatoes are cooked. Pour in milk and season to taste. Heat until piping hot but not boiling.

REINDEER SAUSAGE SOUP

½ pound of reindeer sausage, sliced
1 quart of chicken stock
3 sweet potatoes, peeled and sliced
2 cups of heavy cream
2 tart green apples, peeled, cored & diced
1 onion, diced
2 cloves of garlic, minced
2 tablespoons of oil
Salt and pepper to taste
Tabasco or Frank's Red Hot sauce to taste

Heat oil in a large pot the add onion and garlic. Sauté for 8 to 10 minutes, until onion is softened. Stir in apples, sweet potatoes and chicken stock. Cover and simmer until vegetables are soft, 35 to 40 minutes. Add in cream and mix thoroughly then stir in sausage and cook for 10 minutes. Stir in hot sauce, salt and pepper to taste.

SALMON CHOWDER

2 pounds of salmon, canned or fresh
15 ounces of creamed corn
12 ounces of evaporated milk
8 ounces of cheddar cheese, shredded
2 cups of potatoes, diced
2 cups of chicken broth
2 carrots, diced
¾ cup of onion, diced
½ cup of celery, diced
3 tablespoons of butter
1 teaspoon of garlic powder
1 teaspoon of salt
1 teaspoon of pepper
1 teaspoon of dill

Melt butter in a large pot. Sauté onion, celery and garlic powder over medium heat until onions are tender. Stir in broth, potatoes, carrots, salt, pepper and dill. Bring to a boil and reduce heat. Cover and simmer for 20 minutes. Cut salmon into pieces or flakes. Add the salmon, evaporated milk, corn and cheese. Cook until thoroughly heated.

SALMON RUB

¼ cup of dried orange peel
¼ cup of brown sugar, packed firmly
¼ cup of peppercorns
3 tablespoons of coriander seeds
2 tablespoons of cracked star anise
1 tablespoon of cumin seeds
1 tablespoon of fennel seeds
1 tablespoon of sea salt

Combine all the ingredients in a spice grinder and process to a semi-course texture. Store in an airtight bottle or jar.

SAUTEED MOREL MUSHROOMS

24 morel mushrooms
¾ cup of flour
½ cup of buttermilk
2 tablespoons of oil
2 tablespoons of butter
½ teaspoon of salt
¼ teaspoon of oregano
¼ teaspoon of sugar
¼ teaspoon of garlic powder
White pepper to taste

Quickly rinse mushrooms and drain moisture from the mushrooms before cooking. Combine salt, pepper, flour, oregano, garlic powder and sugar. Cut the dry morels lengthwise. Dip the mushrooms in buttermilk and then dredge in the flour mixture. Melt butter and oil in a large skillet. Sauté mushrooms over medium high heat until crisp and brown on both sides.

SEAFOOD QUICHE

1 pound of shrimp, crab or lobster
1 unbaked pie shell, 9 or 10-inches
3 eggs, beaten
1½ cups of milk or cream
1¼ cups of cheese, grated
1 tablespoon of green pepper, diced fine
1 teaspoon of onion, diced fine
Salt and pepper to taste

Scald milk or cream. Stir in cheese until melted. Add remaining ingredients and mix thoroughly. Slowly pour into the shell. Bake at 350 degrees for 45 minutes or until it sets up firm.

SESAME HALIBUT STEAKS

4 halibut steaks, 1¼-inches thick
8 teaspoons of butter
4 cups of soft breadcrumbs
4 tablespoons of sesame seeds, toasted
4 ounces of butter, melted
1¼ teaspoons of salt
½ teaspoon of thyme
¼ teaspoon of pepper
4 pinches of salt

Place fish in a buttered baking dish. Sprinkle each steak with a pinch of salt and 2 teaspoons of melted butter. Combine remaining ingredients thoroughly and top each piece of fish. Bake at 350 degrees for 24 to 28 minutes or until fish flakes easily.

SHEEP BURGERS

1 pound of ground sheep meat
1 tablespoon of oil
4 slices of bacon, diced
1 teaspoon of salt
Pepper to taste (optional)
4 hamburger buns

Heat oil in a skillet. Mix meat, bacon, salt and pepper thoroughly. Form into 4 ½-inch thick patties. Fry in the skillet on both sides are browned, usually 3 to 5 minutes per sides depending on desired doneness. NEVER push down on the patties. It squeezes out the juice and dries out the meat.

SITKA TEA

1 quart of cranberries, fresh or frozen
3 quarts of water
2 cups of orange juice
   (fresh squeezed if possible)
2 cups of sugar
¼ cup of lemon juice
1 cinnamon stick

In a pan, combine water, cranberries and cinnamon stick. Simmer for 20 to 25 minutes until the berries are tender. Strain the juice through cheesecloth. Toss the residual berry pulp on the compost pile. Mix strained berry juice with lemon juice, orange juice and sugar. Put the mixture in a pan and heat until sugar is dissolved. Serve while still hot. This recipe also works with blueberries, blackberries and raspberries.

SMOKED OYSTER SPREAD

3 ounces of cream cheese, softened
4 ounces of smoked oysters, chopped
2 tablespoons of mayonnaise
1 tablespoon of cream
1 teaspoon of onion, diced fine

Whisk cream cheese in a bowl until a little fluffy. Stir in the rest of the ingredients thoroughly. Chill for 4 hours before serving.

SMOKED STEELHEAD DIP

4 ounces of smoked steelhead, flaked
1/3 cup of heavy cream
½ teaspoon of caper
Black pepper, fresh ground (optional)

Place the fish, cream and capers in a blender until smooth. When ready to serve, sprinkle with pepper.

SOUDOUGH STARTER

2 cups of all-purpose flour
2 cups of warm distilled water

Mix flour and water together in a glass or ceramic bowl. Cover loosely with a towel or cheesecloth and let rest in a warm place for 48 hours. When the mixture is slightly bubbly and sour smelling, stir the mixture, cover and store in the refrigerator. To keep your starter going, feed it every 2 to 3 weeks with 1 cup of water and 1 cup of flour. As you take dough for use, replace with the same amount. The dough should be a pale yellow and white. If it changes to any other color it's time to throw it out.

SOURDOUGH STARTER II

2½ cups of warm milk
2 cups of flour
1 package of dry yeast
2 tablespoons of sugar

Stir yeast, milk and sugar together until yeast is dissolved. Stir in flour gradually until the batter is smooth. Cover loosely with a towel and let stand for 3 to 5 days in a warm spot. Stir down the batter occasionally. When completed, store in the refrigerator with a loose cover.

SOURDOUGH STARTER III

4 cups of sifted flour
1 quart of water
1 package of yeast
2 tablespoons of sugar

In a large crock, soften the yeast with lukewarm water. Add in the sugar and sifted flour and mix thoroughly. Cover and let rise for a day or two. Starter can be stored in the refrigerator for 7 to 10 days without touching it. Then it should be stirred with equal amounts of flour and water added. To maintain the starter, pour off what you need and add equal amounts of water and flour until well blended and batter is smooth.

SPICED WALNUTS

8 ounces of walnut pieces
¼ cup of light corn syrup
¼ cup of butter
2 tablespoons of water
1 teaspoon of cinnamon
½ teaspoon of ground nutmeg
½ teaspoon of ground cloves
Dash of salt

In a pan, combine all ingredients except the walnuts. Bring to a boil over medium heat. Remove the pan from the heat and stir in walnuts. Coat completely. Place the nuts on a cookie sheet and bake at 250 degrees for 1 hour.

STEAMED CLAMS

4 dozen clams in their shells
2 cups of boiling water
Melted butter
Salt

Wash clams thoroughly then cover with cold water. Add ½ cup of salt to each gallon of water. Let clams rest for 15 minutes. Rinse and salt 2 more times. Put clams in a large pot or kettle, add water and bring to a boil. Cover, reduce heat and steam for 10 minutes or until clams open. Drain the clams. Serve hot in shells with melted butter.

STEAMED MUSSELS

4 dozen mussels, well scrubbed
1 cup of white wine
2 scallions, diced
½ teaspoon of thyme
4 dried bay leaves

Place everything in a large pot over high heat. Bring to a boil. Cover and steam for 20 minutes. If there doesn't seem to me enough liquid, add a little more wine.

STEELHEAD FILLETS

2 pounds of steelhead fillets
1 cup of crushed crackers
  (or bread crumbs, cornmeal or Panko)
½ cup of butter
Lemon pepper
Onion salt
Mayonnaise
Italian seasoning
Seafood seasoning
Dill weed

Put fish in a baking dish. Sprinkle fillet with onion salt. Spread mayonnaise over fillet. Sprinkle with Italian seasoning and dill. Next, sprinkle cracker crumbs over fish. Pour melted butter next and top with lemon pepper and seafood seasoning. Bake at 350 degrees for 20 minutes.

STURGEON FILLETS

1½ pounds of sturgeon fillets
¼ cup of flour
½ cup of sherry
½ cup of heavy cream
1 tablespoon of butter
1 tablespoon of oil
½ teaspoon of butter
¼ teaspoon of pepper

Mix flour with salt and pepper. Dust the fish fillets with the flour mixture. Heat butter and oil in a skillet over medium high heat. Cook fillets in the pan for 4 to 6 minutes per side, depending on thickness. After cooking, pour off liquid from the skillet and mix with cream and sherry. Cook the sauce over medium heat until it is reduce by a quarter to a third. Keep fish warm in the oven on low heat with a foil cover. Serve sauce on the side or pour over fish.

SWEET SOY SAUCE

1 ½ cups of soy sauce
½ cup of dark molasses
2 tablespoons of honey
2 tablespoons of lemon juice
1 tablespoon of ginger, fresh grated

Combine all of the ingredients in a pan over medium heat. Bring to a boil and reduce heat to low. Continue cooking until the volume of the sauce is reduced by half. Strain the liquid through cheesecloth or fine mesh. Store in a clean bottle in the refrigerator.

TERIYAKI SALMON

4 salmon steaks
1½ cups of soy sauce
¼ cup of sherry
6 tablespoons of sugar
3 cloves of garlic, minced
1 tablespoon of fresh ginger, grated

Mix soy sauce, sherry, sugar, garlic and ginger together thoroughly. Marinate fish in the sauce for 2 hours in the refrigerator, turning the fish after 1 hour. Barbecue fish on medium heat, basting as you go. When the fish flakes it is done, approximately 17 to 23 minutes.

VENISON STEW

2 pounds of venison, cut into pieces
20 ounces of tomato sauce
2 onions, diced large
3 carrots, diced large
1 can of corn
1 clove of garlic, minced
4 potatoes, cubed
2 tablespoons of black pepper
1 tablespoon of salt
1 tablespoon of celery salt

Combine all ingredients in a large pan and cover. Cook over low to heat for 40 to 45 minutes. Do not let it boil. Once ingredients are tender, remove lid and simmer until it thickens.

VENISON WITH MUSHROOMS

2 pounds of venison
1 can of mushroom soup
1 can of water
1 can of mushrooms, sliced
Flour
Oil
Salt and pepper to taste

Slice the meat into thin strips, dredge in flour and brown with a little oil in a Dutch oven. Once the venison is browned, add 1 can of mushroom soup, 1 can of water and 1 can of mushrooms. Cover the oven and simmer for 1 ½ to 2 hours. Stir frequently to avoid scorching.

WASHINGTON APPLE PANCAKES

2 cups of flour
1 teaspoon of soda
1 tablespoon of sugar
1 teaspoon of salt
½ teaspoon of ground cinnamon
2 eggs
2 cups of buttermilk
¼ cup of butter
1 apple, peeled, cored and grated

In bowl 1 mix together flour, soda, sugar, salt and cinnamon. In bowl 2 mix together eggs, buttermilk, butter and apple. Mix the dry ingredients into the wet to moisten. If batter is too thick, use milk to thin. Drop batter onto a hot griddle. When bubbles appear, flip pancake. Pancakes are done when they are golden brown. Works well with whole wheat flour too.

WILD GAME BARBECUE SAUCE

1½ cups of hot water
1 teaspoon of mustard
1 cup of tomato sauce
1 onion, diced fine
1 clove of garlic, diced fine
½ cup of celery, diced
Juice of 1 lemon
1 tablespoon of Worcestershire sauce
1 teaspoon of lemon zest
¼ teaspoon of Tabasco sauce
¼ teaspoon of thyme
3 bay leaves

In a pot, mix all ingredients thoroughly. Cover and cook on low for 2 to 3 hours. If it is too thick, add a little more water. This recipe can also be made in a slow cooker set on medium low. Stir mixture once an hour. Remove bay leaves when it is fully cooked.

WINTER STEW

2 pounds of beef, venison, elk or moose meat, cubed
3 onions, diced
3 carrots, sliced
2 potatoes, diced
1 stalk of celery, diced
1 cup of water
1 clove of garlic, minced
1 teaspoon of Worcestershire sauce
1 tablespoon of salt
1 teaspoon of paprika
½ teaspoon of pepper
1 bay leaf
Flour

Lightly dust the beef cubes with flour and brown in a skillet. Put beef in a slow cooker followed by vegetables and water. Stir to mix. Now add spices and stir just enough to mix well. Cover the cooker and cook on low for 10 to 12 hours.

For more information on the entire series of Tim Murphy's "Cookbooks for Guys" and his other book projects, visit www.flanneljohn.com.

Made in the USA
Columbia, SC
23 November 2020